MEMENTO MORI

MEMENTO MORI

SHORT POEMS FOR A SHORT LIFE

∞

SCOTT F. PARKER

SYNTHESIS PUBLICATIONS

MMXXV

Printed in the United States of America.

First edition, 2025.

ISBN 979-8-218-72111-4

Grateful acknowledgment is made to those publications where many of these poems first appeared: *Shadow Pond Journal, Cold Moon Journal, 5-7-5 Haiku Journal, FreshOut Mag, Presence, 5haikuSpoken, Hedgerow, Acorn, Alien Buddha Zine, Triya,* and *Trash Panda.*

scottfparker.com

for the mortal

after the rain
all the happy grass
waving in the wind

lost in the orchard
in no hurry to be found—
poems grow on trees

three friends
bottle of wine
first evening of summer

my beautiful boys
asleep in the summer grass
growing in the sun

summer solstice:
Bozeman
like a picture of Bozeman

running on the beach
a lone seagull
looking for the flock

miles of sand
each step
sinking in

the toddler
watching the gulls
lift off

the orange-pink sun
falls into the summer sea
not even a splash

by the running creek
shaded from the summer sun
the afternoon rests

my boy at the creek
touching stick to rock, writing
haiku in water

gray house
in the rain:
no one home

afternoon shadows
chasing children
across the yard

fresh pile of elk shit
marking the path of decay
we are following

dead tree over there
alone in the green forest—
I see you see me

one summer sunrise
this old world still here
leaves on the trees

a sliver of moon
and the mist at Ousel Falls
as the day begins

on my face
waterfall mist
touching sunburn

window open
the sound of rain—
I sleep like a child

another rainy day
away
from smoke season

brittle blue sky
holding still
against the ridge

floating on the water
hawk
through the empty sky

being on the water
with my son
and ten thousand suns

not after Basho

even in Bozeman—
on a cloudy summer day—
I long for Portland

blue sky
white clouds—
paddling over them

forty thousand bees
coming and going—
the hive stays put

lonely trail
through the desert at sunrise
smell of sage

son to my father
as the summer grass grows
father to my sons

summer evening
pink sky
with wife

summer breeze—
lying out in the sun
a small snake

another nap
another poem
not written

the low of a cow
like a Richard Wright haiku
I read this morning

pink ball in the sky
where the sun should be
this smoky morning

wind blowing smoke
so thick
the mountains go too

the trail leads the way
the only way—
to the end of the trail

whooshing falls
turnaround point—
end of summer

in memory of Sarah Cook

I saw you today
in a stranger's face, two months
since you have been gone

after Basho

the start of autumn
appearing
in the tips of aspen leaves

with Parker J. Newton

rainy soccer practice
all the boys drenched
in laughter

plenty of room
in the day
for rain

after Nick Virgilio

my sons and I
with no footprints to follow
leave our own trail

black coffee
this morning
with clouds

senseless war
senseless life
my beautiful boys

Oregon—
I just like the way it sounds
like more again

it was all a dream
even the dream was a dream
said the god of dreams

memento mori
the day after tomorrow
is already here

memento mori
the green bloom of aspen trees
will be over soon

memento mori
the Latin language is dead—
what is there to say?

memento mori
the song won't last forever
but it's playing now

memento mori
day after day after day
you must change your life

pelican in flight
father and son looking on
and then it's over

morning walk to school
hawk on the telephone pole—
take good notes, student

leaky pen in hand
thoughts spilling over the page
as the ink runs out

the thought of Eugene
and the smell of rainy days
linger near the soul

mug warm with coffee
no rain
yet falling

old man praying
to the god
of his youth

fish by the shore
fisherman by the shore
across the pond

father and son chess—
the implacable king watching
the opposing army approach

two cougar cubs
creeping silently out
of the photo on the wall

big nighttime silence
immense nighttime sky
this one small life

hungry cat
leaves footprints
in notebook again

at one with nature
reading old books
on the computer

empty porch swing
rocking
at dusk

prairie grass
two sandhill cranes
and our stopped car

fast-running creek—
the thrown rock
makes no sound

coffee and donuts
as I police
the sunrise

soggy newspaper
forecasts
more rain

sunrise
the silence
of a dead rooster

my old sweatshirt
looking better than ever
on my wife's shoulders

the weight of him
in my lap reading stories
this morning

rainy evening
invisible tears

walking alone
in the woods
not seeing a cougar

the mountain stream
and the bridge crossing it
to the other side

by the lake
trees and mountains
holding up the sky

after Ruby Spriggs

growth in the children
in the garden
in the universe

the same books
year after year
waiting to be read

after Basho

as for the mouse
in the backyard—
the cat standing by

where we are—
beyond us
only fog

learning to walk
on the beach
straight for the sea

outside my window
and inside it too—
the universe

this house cat
she's in middle age
unless she's not

stranger in the mirror
strange only to a ghost
I guess I believe in

two deer
just off the busy trail
minding their business

hawk on lamppost
two hawks on lamppost
no hawks on lamppost

fingers touching
in my lap
in consciousness

the nature of self—
why do we ask such questions?
and who wants to know?

no directions needed
to the path
beneath my feet

turtles on the shore
keeping busy
maintaining stillness

a short poem
about the lake and the moose
I didn't see there

life is what happens
while you are busy waiting
for coffee to brew

mix coffee with books
let sit twenty or more years—
results may vary

a field of mushrooms
sprouts overnight
alongside magic

avoiding death
the old man
he died anyway

for eleven years
the cat sits on the man's lap
then suddenly jumps down

news of a friend's death
finds me early one morning
looking at the stars

the falling leaf lands
at the feet of a young child
who stops to notice

I remember Europe—
reading Dostoevsky
on a cobblestone bridge

nighttime silence
overwhelming
the voices in my head

winter twilight:
a crow alights
in my mind

black cat
purring
in the dark room

the sound of stars
in the nighttime sky
if you listen closely

awake in the night
the snow outside
reflecting moonlight

just another day
coming to an end
lone bison in the cold

the sun goes first
followed by the mountain
& eventually me

for Natalie Goldberg

writing practice
uncovering the bones
of the self

photograph of an owl
as real to me
as I am to myself

morning moonlight—
the snowy field
cast in blue

winter silence
returns
as coyote howls fade

middle of the night
confronting the mysteries
I can see like stars

black rabbit
white snow
simple picture

winter morning—
the silent moon lost
to a silent cloud

after Lorainne Ellis Harr

the time it takes—
for the moon to disappear
behind clouds

January snow
God all in the alpenglow—
something in me melts

another cold day:
somewhere in my journey
the smell of springtime

after Jack Johnson

the stars and the sky
belong to each other and
both belong to me

compared to Issa
the dawn
is a little bland

no one
likes long poems
anyway

baby's first steps
like spring flowers
suddenly manifest

dozing in the spring
waking up
in a new dream

the future is here
says the sweatshirt Wing gave to
the boys who wear it

oldest woman I've loved—
        older
    every year

127

another spring comes
write your poems while you may
another spring goes

the scent of roses
my childhood returns like that
but returns from where?

woodpecker
drilling a hole
to the center of attention

life—
the sun rises
I don't ask why

walking in the rain
conversation lasting
so far a life

each drop of rain
assuring me
we've met before

the way green
gets even greener
in late spring

all the wild animals
that have walked
this empty path

today's rain washing away yesterday's

war poverty disease
and trees sprouting up
like children

under the log—
not the snake
I imagined

cougar noticing
you not noticing
cougar

my dear sons—
corpses
in the making

ideas everywhere I turn
& beyond them
the world

pasture gate latched
on either side
no fence

www.ingramcontent.com/pod-product-compliance
Lightning Source LLC
Chambersburg PA
CBHW032037040426
42449CB00007B/919